The Witness of Life: Humanity

Cindy Huynh

BookLeaf
Publishing

The Witness of Life: Humanity © 2023

Cindy Huynh

All rights reserved.

No part of this publication may be reproduced, stored in a retrieval system, or transmitted, in any form or by any means, electronic, mechanical, photocopying, recording or otherwise, without the prior written permission of the presenters.

Cindy Huynh asserts the moral right to be identified as author of this work.

Presentation by *BookLeaf Publishing*

Web: www.bookleafpub.com

E-mail: info@bookleafpub.com

ISBN: 9789357696036

First edition 2023

After Lunch Break

It was a Tuesday Afternoon
Waiting together with my sister in line
Nothing special about the mood
We were just there for a typical deadline

Closer to the front of the line
A worker came back to her seat
The first resident she service to was not fine
He puts a simple question to heat

The resident was rude and dramatic
He uses others waiting in line as an excuse for his
impatience
To his side, a helper initiates to lecture the
problematics
To the helper's dismay, the rude man ignores her
request of compliance

We look into each other's eyes and communicate
Poor worker had to start her afternoon with a disaster
I looked into her upsetting eyes and wish the
atmosphere can rejuvenate
Lucky for me I brought her a big sunshine when I had
her soon after

The witness of life, no one have not seen before
Simply to say, have you witness before
Afternoons are not easy anymore
In life, it is the difficult core

The Brave TA (teaching assistant)

It was the same hour of the week
Sitting with my comfy clothes on
I scored one less class for the streak
Waiting for the longest hour to move along

In the middle of the online tutorial
The mood is dead silent when questions arrive
Discouraged, she suggests the worst fear of students
Immediately, I scrambled the internet for materials
Again, the class is ambient, but she gave in and we survived
As class finalize, she was happy to see the improvements

Although the changes were minor
At least the students were trying
It is stressful enough to be the tutor
Let alone, the leader who is crying

The witness of life, the fear of speaking
At the least, especially when pleasing
Participation is important in all kinds of meeting
Regardless of listening, providing, or leading

A Smile for Food

On a very hungry time of day, two little pigs were
starving
One of the pigs got off the wheels and went into the
store
The little pig waits behind a big line for food
shopping.
The little pig orders one box and the cook walks
away but she wants more.

The little pig watches the cook rush through their
sweats
The little pig watches as others behind her pays for
their box
The cook becomes the cashier but little pig said
there's more to get
The cashier sighs, takes the order and becomes a
feisty chef fox

After a while, the feisty fox becomes the cashier
again
The cashier puts the food in the slippery bag and
hands it to the little pig
The cashier greets the pig to enjoy her meal and the
little pig smiles and drain
Back to the wheels, the little pig takes small breaks as
the bag is hard to rig

Back into their cold home, little pig opens her box
and sighs
Little pig takes a few slurps and gives up, pouring it
into a bowl
The content is tasteless, wet, sloppy, like a slump of
dump
Little pig lost her appetite, but is hungry and wants to
cry
In the end, she slurps and slurps and she feels a little
whole
Yet, it took the little pig hours to finish her lump of
clump

The witness of life, we have all experienced
Regardless of service, not all will be delicious
Especially when the store is at its busiest
One hungry pig can only resilience

Can You Spare a few Change

It was a typical warm day of a bizarre season
Under the mask, no way I will not sweat or be short
of breath
My face is bursting in flames and ice I will squeeze
in
A high enriched cafe store I see before my death

In line I begin standing, and loud music I hear
I hesitate in guilt of what I should request
A drink for money or a drink for guilt, I am near
"An ice water please," for this hideous guest

The cashier turns into a barista and becomes my hero
In seconds she return with a free cup of water
I thank her for charging me zero
Everyone deserves it and it is never a botter

I walked away with my spare of change
Others were still waiting for their beautiful crafts
A sip I take and now I'm a renowned daughter
A daughter who found kindness in others

The witness of life, we all hope to see more
Simply to say, it should not be a botter
Neither should one feel guilty for knocking on the
door
A simple action will make everyone's day better

Four Crisis of a Meal

It's good they say, it's top notch they say
But will what they say, match our level
Our level is simple, something that sparks yay
And that is how we met the devil

We walked in and bump into a familiar face
We sit down with high expectations
They took our orders and off we wait
Waiting, it definitely was a disgrace
Mine arrived first and looks like a sensation
It looks like a perfect vase that cannot be replaced

A few minutes in arrives my mother's dish
She couldn't wait and began chugging
Dad is pretending everything is okay
But then takes a few sips of mine and more after
Finally his arrived at last, looking less than a wish
He asked for garnish as none was coming
A cold piece of meat, he is betrayed

All of our dish were filled with orange looking soup
At least we decided not to get take out for our
beloved
As it was a very disrupting group of poop
Did not complain as the place is flooded

The witness of life, something we cannot avoid
There's nothing we can do as we know it is not their
fault
Especially when we give it too high of a hope
At least we learn from our mistakes and not to come
again

Birthday Equality

What is someone's birthday to me
It is when one is rewarded for existence
It is also when one have survived a year-long journey
Not to mention, one's deserving equality of desires

What is someone's birthday to me
It is when people go easier on your mistakes
It is also when your loved ones help you celebrate
Not to mention, one's moment of taking advantages

What is someone's birthday to me
It is when one gets discounts and free gifts
It is also when people roll their eyes at you
Not to mention, being blamed for the things asked

What is someone's birthday to me
It is when one cannot afford a cake
It is also when one cries and eat alone
Not to mention, one's knowledge that no one
remembers their birthday

What is someone's birthday to me
It is the witness of life that we simply cannot ignore
Whether that one life is alive or not to the day one
remembers
Especially when one have impacted another
individual greatly

The Core of Bus Fares

The days are getting darker faster
I come out of the building to a breath of fresh air
Only to realize the chilly atmosphere and the
disasters
How is taking the bus alone fair

I take out my phone and instantly dial a call
"Are you here yet?" I asked my darling sister
Walking further down towards the hall
A car honked as loud as the touch of a blister

There I see, my darling sister and Wall-EE
Wall-EE is a gorgeous white hybrid robot
And I am excited to be the last customer for the night
So there goes my dancing legs and shivering body
Hopping onto the seat and thanking sister for her
support
As we also get to communicate and reunite

In under ten minutes we arrived home
Somewhere safe and sound from the cold
At least I did not have to go through the unknown
Where mysterious strangers and anxiety unfolds

The witness of life, we have all seek help for
Someone to carpool and save money with time
Simply for security and priorities measures
And thanking individuals for their help and benign

The Kindness of Joy

I woke up to the late hours of noon
Grumpy and angry of all the sounds I hear
Which no longer appear when I hear typhoon
The sounds of my hungriness that I cannot bare

After refilling my dangerous medications, I reformed
into a chef
A chef with two pots and dancing tunes on
Spicing the water with sauce and powder to assess
Extracting some liquid results to burning steam of
songs

I blow onto my hand and continue to cook
My sister offers to do the dishes after the meal
Jumped of joy I begin eating the time I took
Ensuring no one complains, she also offered to wash
grandpa's steels

I sit through the meal of no pressure
I sit through noon with no one complaining of the
dishes
I sit through the hour absorbing treasures
Wondering what made my sister want to do the
dishes

The witness of life, something call love and support
Someone who acknowledges your values and state of
mind
Simply to say, someone who cares about your
significance
Or returns the favour of being grateful for the
delicious food

The Reward of a Helping Hand

It was a dark evening at the mall
Although I wouldn't be able to tell
My dad and I we walked and walked
Until the very end when I sense their smell

I walked in with a paper bag of their logo
They thought I was here for trouble
But I wasn't here for any photo
I'm just waiting in line being flexible

From the bag I began taking out glass bottles
One, two, three, and soon to the very bottom
"I am here to collect points" I gobbled
Unfortunately they had a new system causing
problem

The internet was slow and I was very upset
I came all the way here just to return some bottles
She looked me in the eyes and says "don't fret"
"I will give you coins instead," says the model

I was excited to receive one dollar and a quarter
My dad looked into my palms and was disappointed
"I brought you all the way here just for quarters?"
At least it wasn't coins stuck in a system of poignant.

The witness of life, there's always a solution
Even when you give up filled with tears
As long as you keep trying to do your best
Someone out there will acknowledge your dedication.

The Care of Details

It was a warm day in bed and soon arrives noon
I was craving for a specific food of a specific restaurant
There I go, ordering online as if I have nothing else to do
Through the process, I also listed what I don't want

Moments later my sister drove me to the adorable place
A place that I considered comfortable to enjoy a meal
A place where there is just enough eating space
A place where cash discount becomes a steal

We arrived home and instantly I opened the take out
To my surprise, they listened to my request
A request that I thought would cause doubts
The care of details made me very blessed

Flavours of the spicy udon at the tip of my tongue
An aroma of touch that I could never forget
As if my palette lost touch and into the air it swung
Making every bite transform into sweat

The witness of life, when attention to details becomes a
bonus
Especially when they do as requested of special instructions
And even better when the taste is above and beyond
Now that is a kind of chef who cares about customer's
satisfaction

An Action of Remembrance

Once upon a time a little girl had to stay silent
She never ask why but believes it was important
Every same day of the month is the same assignment
Sitting in the assembly hosted by the informant

As the years go by, the same type of assembly continues
But the informant may deliver the news differently
Some may do it more creatively to result in less tissues
Regardless, every assembly always ends coherently

Now that I've outgrown from the requirements of
attendment
I've realize how much I missed learning about the issues
Thus the part of honour and respect through sentiment
With a small pin of poppy in expectation of remembrance
and reuse

Although there are times when newcomers will question
the event
And the times when one may forget the proper explanations
One would always remember regardless when the time is
intent
And there will be ways to form a sense of reflection

The witness of life, it can be hard at times
Lest we forget, those who stand before us
Even if we may not know who they are
We will always try our best just because

Should I Feel Guilty

Should I feel Guilty
For the unsatisfied belly near the end of midnight
For the want of craving fast food
Not to mention, the discounts in the mail

Should I feel Guilty
For the delivery man who delivered to the wrong house
For the customer who never got their food delivered
Not to mention, founded right by my doorside

Should I feel Guilty
For bringing the food in to avoid animals
For the staring at the bucket of cold fries
Not to mention, the inclusion of a whole meal

Should I feel Guilty
For taking something that doesn't belong to me
For waiting anxiously for the return of the delivery man
Not to mention, the possibility of the customer knocking on
my door

Should I feel Guilty
The witness of life that I simply cannot control
Especially when its sitting right in front of me
Even my family could not hold it in
Thank you for the free meal and sorry for the pleasure
But your address was nowhere to be found
Only the sounds of a hungry belly

The Cost Per Utensils

On a fine Sunday afternoon, three little monkeys were
hungry
Hungry enough that they were struggling to choose where
to eat
The places they looked for were filled and soon the
monkeys were grumpy
At last the three monkeys found a food court with many
seats

Waiting for the food, there were too many seats to choose
from
One monkey got up from the seat and walked to another
store
The other monkey hops to get food as it comes
While the tiny monkey sits and cannot wait anymore

Before eating, one monkey goes up and ask for an extra
plate
"That will be a quarter," chef alligator says as she rolls her
eyes
The sad monkey walks back to the seat and translate
Together the three monkeys take turn with each of the
supplies

Soon after the tiny monkey comes up with a suggestion
Perhaps this rule should have applied with the plastic
straws
For that would have paper straws be in discussion
At last we were happy once and for all

The witness of life, a social issue that we all have seen
before
Perhaps if one took this to consideration would it have
changed
For the better of the world that people continue to ignore
Especially when it has become a habit that is hard to be
contained

The Feelings of a Punching Bag

It was a Monday afternoon
Waiting for the owl in arrival
As I sit in an empty classroom
Waiting to the end of the cycle

The owl reaches beyond the door
And I pronounce a form of greet
Only to be ignored like corps
And seeing her respond to the next repeat

At some point I decided to share some news
Again the owl ignored my call and response in hurry
At some point I did a task as I am always there to be cued
There goes the owl complaining I set the lights off too early

At another point, the owl thought I was mad
But to their surprise, I did my task again
At last it all went well yet I was very sad
Only in hopes to not get criticized at again

The witness of life, for being put on the spot
Yet, everyone knew you did nothing wrong
It was the matter of someone's mood
Which we simply should forgive the honk

The Request of Time

As I continue to stress through my notes
A notification roared through the air
Scrolling through the obvious of a boat
A friend of mine is ready to declare

Following her roars, I went online to the site
Soon after reaching many questions ahead
Trying my best to help I pray it will end
At last I could no longer hold my invite
Only to splurged my annoyance instead
All I wanted was to help a friend

My dear friend have given up in despair of
Remembering the importance of my studies
So insisted for the request of another hand
Thus made me upset of my impatient stress
Yet I hope I can offer my expertise above
But will have to be delayed to be buddies
Filled with love who would understand

Thereafter, a request of feedback with a survey
Not every human on earth will have the patience
Neither will anyone be easily attracted to its display
But would a feedback of our time be efficacious

The witness of life, it will always appear on the receipt
Whether it came from shopping for clothes or buying food
It is a piece of paper that we can easily trash under our feet
But perhaps it is time to reconsider the value to include

The Helper of the House

Silly this is but I must say in peace
For that if she did not, no one would know
She opens the door and there it release
If not removed it would continue to grow

She comes in and starts complaining
For that we went through a fierceful debate
At last we found out the truth of dumping
It was the radish liquid in the mixture of fate

We waited and waited and I just give in
Walking near the car I take a deep breath
Open to the door of disaster I grabbed the bag
Letting my nose scent the cold weather I regret

Indeed it was the empty bag of vomit scents
Nothing inside except a small cup of radish sauce
For that I hope the car will sleep and not vent
As I hurry back into the house filled with thoughts

The witness of life, we've all smelled before
Whether it is at home or on the street
Even when it is in a restaurant or in a mall
For that a soul filled with greatness for those
Who have provided us all a better environment

Patience is Key

Not long ago have this hobby started
Something more like taking chances
Something that could be supported
Something that could help finance

I'm very fortunate for my participation
Assisting my father in every way I can
To ensure my skills helps his reputation
For that I am proud of what have began

Although at times I get frustrated
For the time he made me waste
For the workload that I have donated
For the stress that I have faced

Now that I've been renowned the assistant
I can finally take my advantage of skills
And at times be compensated for my existence
Through the efficiency of what I have built

The witness of life, every effort aims to be
acknowledged
For that I shall not be disappointed
Even if it takes longer than expected
To be rewarded for what I have amounted

The Impulsive Buyer

What time is it
It is the time to get into the festivities
It it the time to start planning for gifts
Not to mention, the time to budget

What time is it
It is the time to face your greatest fear
It is the time to start counting down
Not to mention, the time of self-control

What time is it
It is the time you might just go broke
It is the time where you have a list
Not to mention, the time to organize

What time is it
It is the time to reflect on yourself
It is the time to acknowledge others
Not to mention, those you loathe as well

What time is it
The witness of life, we have all struggled to avoid
However, it is also a time we all hope to offer
In relation to the amounts of gifts we can afford
For those we want to thank, love, and appreciate

The Headache of Tips

Somewhere between morning and noon
A call it takes to get your stomach full
Hurried to traffic as the food will arrive soon
Stepping on the brakes before the place is booked

Arriving at the lot we looked for a spot
A spot for Ruby the car to take a restful break
Soon after we enter the place on the dot
And wait in line for what sweets to take

Ten dishes of a goodness
Something dripping down my lips
Asking how much to pay for its kindness
Before I unveiled and tear the smell I rip

I don't got a loonie but I have a toonie
Thanking for the speed, an extra dollar as tip
There we go, leaving the meals to me
And letting my legs holding onto its grip

The witness of life, we've all hesitate before
Whether we should tip for only in place or take out as well
When offered the question, just give it a go
Better to appreciate than ending with an upsetting face

The Hunger of a Human

Some people call it morning
Some people call it noon
Some people call it in between
Some people even call it to the moon

I waited an hour or two
But there are no response of where is the food
My head hurts of stress as hunger is due
I am grumpy as if noodle isn't any good

After a couple of runs through my head
I give up and decided noodle is what I'll have instead
Although its taste of texture is like a plain bread
At least my hungry stomach will be fed.

During the process of slurping the spicy soup
I acknowledged the gain of my favourite spice
Only to realize I should be grateful for the group
Thus the love and support was never a price

The witness of life, not everyone will be granted for it
Only those of luck were able to accomplish it
Which is why we should not complain of what we have
As others of less fortunate cannot be compared

The Kindness of Power

Winter holidays are flashing before my eyes
So I thought I could go for a quick snoop around
To only find a brand of toothbrush to my surprise
Which indeed is my mom's favourite sounds

I grabbed a few and into the lane I went
Only to realize the price stayed the same
I questioned the worker who can represent
To acknowledge manager is his name

Kindly he checked and give me a glance
Informing me that the sale have been sailed
However my eyes begin to shimmer and dance
Once he told me he can give me the sale

From a five to a one I was jumping with joy
He then leaves a sticker on my receipt
Hoping I would offer a feedback for my toy
Indeed I would as he was very sweet

The witness of life, not all will expect
But if you're lucky, perhaps it will come
The life he saved for all that I kept
Not all would appreciate this kind of sum
But I'm fortunate for what it made me become

www.ingramcontent.com/pod-product-compliance
Lightning Source LLC
LaVergne TN
LVHW021354200726

843509LV00014B/2835